D0443964

Walking with the Savior

TYNDALE HOUSE PUBLISHERS,

MAX LUCADO

Walking with the Savior

INCORPORATED, WHEATON, ILLINOIS

Copyright © 1996 by Max Lucado.
All rights reserved.

Quotations from Max Lucado compiled by Karen Hill, previously published in the
Walking with the Savior calendar

Designed by Raelee Edgar

Photography credits:
Wayne Alderidge/International Stock: 159; Josiah Davidson: 22-23, 68,114-115, 121,
152; M. Edwards/International Stock: 51; Chad Ehlers/International Stock: 72-73;
Ric Ergenbright: Jacket photos, 3, 20-21, 46-47, 58-59, 86-87, 102-103; Christopher
Frank: 26, 32, 43, 64, 79; Dennis Frates: 2, 29, 36, 99, 106-107, 158; I.T.P./Inter-
national Stock: 117; Adam Jones: 16, 53, 94, 115; Mike Magnuson/International
Stock: 142-143; Lynn Stone: 3, 124, 145; Dusty Willison/International Stock: 88.

Paintings from Planet Art:
Bazille: 76; Monet: 2, 8, 13, 39, 48-49, 56-57, 70-71, 104, 128-129, 132, 154-155;
Morris: 30-31, 40-41, 44-45, 54-55, 62, 82, 90-91, 96-97, 118-119, 126-127, 134-
135, 140-141, 150-151; Sargent: 108-109; Seurat: 24-25; Van Gogh: 18-19, 75, 100-
101, 122-123, 138, 146-147, 148-149.

Unless otherwise indicated, Scriptures are taken from the *Holy Bible*, New Century
Version, copyright © 1987, 1988, 1991 by Word Publishing, Dallas, Texas, 75039.
Used by permission.

ISBN 0-8423-7930-4.

01 00 99 98 97 96
 6 5 4 3 2 1

Presented to:

_____

_____

Contents

Living in the Master's Grace

All have sinned and are not good

What is grace? It's what someone gives us out of the

enough for God's glory, and all

goodness of their heart, not out of the perfection of

need to be made right with God

ours. The story of grace is the good news that says

by his grace, which is a free gift.

that when we come, he gives. That's what grace is.

ROMANS 3:23-24

God's love for you is not dependent on how you look, how you think, how you act, or how perfect you are. His love is absolutely nonnegotiable and nonreturnable. Ours is a faithful God.

Holy, holy, holy is the Lord God Almighty.

He was, he is, and he is coming.

REVELATION 4:8

The same Holy Spirit that operates wonderfully inside a person is the exact power that went into a dark tomb where lay the broken and lifeless body of Jesus Christ and somehow, in a way no human being can ever explain, breathed life-giving power into that body.

We know that we live in God and he lives in us, because he gave us his Spirit. . . . Whoever confesses that Jesus is the Son of God has God living inside, and that person lives in God. 1 JOHN 4:13, 15

Your love is wonderful.
By your power you save those who trust you from their enemies.
Protect me as you would protect your own eye.
Hide me under the shadow of your wings.

PSALM 17:7-8

Simply because you can't put your hands around something doesn't mean it's not there. In fact, those things that are most precious to us are the things that are invisible, aren't they? Love, tenderness, happiness, air, feelings, emotions—those things we cannot touch, but they are very real. And so it is with God's power: It may not be touchable, but it's real and it's obtainable.

Jesus described for his followers what he came to do. He came to build relationships with people. He came to take away the enmity, to take away the strife, to take away the isolation that existed between God and man. Once he bridged that, once he overcame that, he said, "I will call you friends."

I no longer call you servants, because a servant does not know what his master is doing.

But I call you friends, because I have made known to you everything I heard from my Father.

JOHN 15:15

Perhaps the words of the Carpenter, promising rest, are so compelling because of our endless desire and quest to rest—not just to rest in the body, but to rest the heart, to find peace, to finally settle down in a valley fertile with contentment.

Come to me, all of you who are tired and have heavy loads, and I will give you rest.
MATTHEW 11:28

What is the grace of God? The grace of God says you serve God because you're saved, not in order to be saved. You love people because you're saved, and not in order to be saved. You're not trying to keep a legalistic system, you're responding to a system of love and peace.

Christ ended

the law so that

everyone who

believes in him

may be right

with God.

ROMANS 10:4

Grace is a pleasant surprise.

Grace is a kind gesture.

Grace is something you did not expect.

It is something you certainly could never earn.

But grace is something you'd never turn down.

Because he was full of grace and truth, from him we all received one gift after another.

JOHN 1:16

Your rules are wonderful. That is why I keep them. Learning your words gives wisdom and understanding for the foolish.

PSALM 119:129-130

When you light somebody afire with the grace of God, you have a hard time putting him out. When you light people with legalism or with rules and regulations, they're going to burn out because they'll always live in fear. But a person set afire with the love of Jesus Christ will live in gratitude—serving his Lord out of love and not out of fear.

Christ gave each one of us the special gift of grace,

showing how generous he is.

EPHESIANS 4:7

The more we are loved by God,

the more we are going to love.

The more we are forgiven,

the more we're willing to forgive.

The more we're treated with patience,

the more we are willing to treat others with patience.

These are all extensions of that gift of grace.

Salvation is the process that's done, that's secure, that no one can take away from you. Sanctification is the lifelong process of being changed from one degree of glory to the next, growing in Christ, putting away the old, taking on the new.

All things are worth nothing compared with the greatness of knowing Christ Jesus my Lord. Because of him, I have lost all those things, and now I know they are worthless trash.

PHILIPPIANS 3:8

Forgiveness of the Father

Sometimes we try to deal with a mistake by covering it up with more mistakes, or by repressing it, or by justifying it. That's like walking around with a pebble in our shoe—it causes us so much frustration that our whole body compensates for its presence, when all we have to do is take it out and toss it away.

Though your sins are like scarlet,
they can be as white as snow.
Though your sins are deep red,
they can be white like wool.   ISAIAH 1:18

Revealing our feelings is the beginning of healing.

Articulating what's on our heart, confessing our

mistakes, is the first step in seeing that God

can forgive those mistakes and all others.

God, examine me and know my heart; test me and know my nervous thoughts.

PSALM 139:23

When we avoid dealing

with our mistakes and

pretend they don't exist,

they usually express

themselves in ways that

we would not anticipate:

anger at someone else,

frustration at something

else, lack of control.

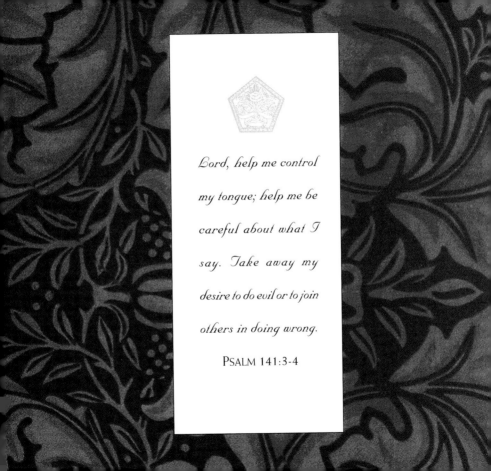

Lord, help me control my tongue; help me be careful about what I say. Take away my desire to do evil or to join others in doing wrong.

PSALM 141:3-4

We don't like to recognize our ruin, but that's where Jesus begins. Once we're honest with ourselves about who we are, then God can begin to remold our hearts . . . total surrender.

But if we confess our sins, he will forgive our sins, because we can trust God to do what is right. He will cleanse us from all the wrongs we have done.
1 JOHN 1:9

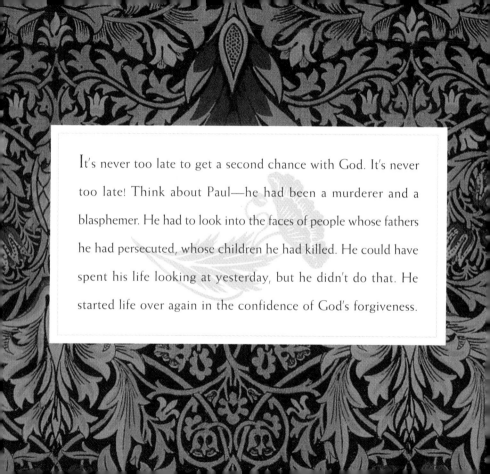

It's never too late to get a second chance with God. It's never too late! Think about Paul—he had been a murderer and a blasphemer. He had to look into the faces of people whose fathers he had persecuted, whose children he had killed. He could have spent his life looking at yesterday, but he didn't do that. He started life over again in the confidence of God's forgiveness.

Lord, you are kind and forgiving
and have great love for those who call to you.

PSALM 86:5

No one is happier than the one who has sincerely repented of wrong. Repentance is the decision to turn from selfish desires and seek God. It is a genuine, sincere regret that creates sorrow and moves us to admit wrong and desire to do better.

On the day I called to you, you answered me. You made me strong and brave.

PSALM 138:3

Does the Word of God say, "There is *limited* condemnation for those who are in Christ Jesus"? No. Does it say, "There is *some* condemnation . . . "? No. It says, "There is *no* condemnation for those who are in Christ Jesus." Think of it—regardless of our sin, we are not guilty!

Through Christ Jesus the law of the Spirit that brings

life made me free from the law that brings sin and death.

ROMANS 8:2

Father in heaven, help us as we grapple and cope with

yesterday's failures. They dog at our heels like irritations.

They follow us around. They cling to our ankles like

fifteen-pound ball weights. Help us to release those

regrets in the right way, and keep us close.

See if there is any bad thing in me. Lead me on the road to everlasting life.

PSALM 139:24

Jesus says, "Use your head, but don't lower your standards." You be the one who interrupts that vicious cycle of paying one another back. Don't get on the roller coaster of resentment and anger. You be the one who says, "Yes, he mistreated me, but I am going to be like Christ. I'll be the one who says, 'Forgive them, Father, they don't know what they're doing.'"

Get along with each other, and forgive each other. If someone does wrong to you, forgive that person because the Lord forgave you.

COLOSSIANS 3:13

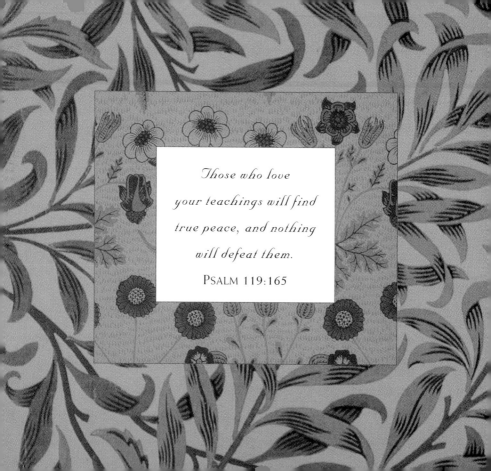

Those who love your teachings will find true peace, and nothing will defeat them.

PSALM 119:165

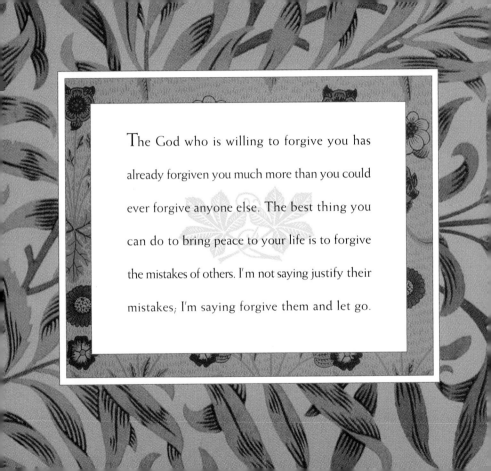

The God who is willing to forgive you has already forgiven you much more than you could ever forgive anyone else. The best thing you can do to bring peace to your life is to forgive the mistakes of others. I'm not saying justify their mistakes; I'm saying forgive them and let go.

*When you are praying, if you are angry
with someone, forgive him so that your Father
in heaven will also forgive your sins.*

MARK 11:25

Isn't it presumptuous to come to the throne of grace if we haven't been gracious to the people in our life? How can we approach a God of mercy if we ourselves have hearts full of bitterness or anger? We must take care of relationship problems—make up with a spouse, get along with fellow church members, love our neighbors—then we will be fully united in prayer with the Father.

But if anyone does sin, we have a helper in the presence of the Father—Jesus Christ, the One who does what is right. He is the way our sins are taken away, and not only our sins but the sins of all people.

1 JOHN 2:1-2

What makes a Christian a Christian is not perfection but forgiveness.

Worshiping the King

Praise is the highest occupation of any being. What happens when we praise the Father? We reestablish the proper chain of command; we recognize that the King is on the throne and that he has saved his people.

Praise the Lord for the glory of his name;
worship the Lord because he is holy.
PSALM 29:2

God, I will thank you forever
for what you have done. With those who worship you,
I will trust you because you are good.

PSALM 52:9

Gratitude comes from having the right perspective. It's
being able to look at what you have and being thankful
for that, rather than longing for what you don't have.

It's incredible that anyone could

look at the kindness of God,

the faithfulness of God, and

the goodness of God and not

feel any emotion of gratitude.

Lord, I will thank you with all my heart; I will sing to you.

PSALM 138:1

We should serve God even if there is darkness enveloping our

I will praise the Lord at all times;

life and even if we don't understand what's happening . . .

his praise is always on my lips.

even when the circumstances of our life don't make sense:

My whole being praises the Lord.

Because he is worthy of praise, Because he is God.

PSALM 34:1-2

Father in heaven, hear our praise. Holy Father, we are thankful that we have more than enough clothes to wear, thankful that we have places to sleep and that we won't go to bed hungry. We're thankful that even if all of this were taken away from us, we'd still have our hope of eternity. You have been gracious to us.

You are worthy, our Lord and God, to receive glory and honor and power, because you made all things. Everything existed and was made, because you wanted it.

REVELATION 4:11

Father, you never promised us that this world would be easy. And yet, all of us can look ahead to the city that's set on a hill, to the lights that call us to eternity. And we take hope.

*His glory covers
the skies, and his
praise fills the earth.
He is like a bright
light. Rays of light
shine from his hand,
and there he hides
his power.*

HABAKKUK 3:3-4

When you take food to the poor,
   that's an act of worship.

When you give a word of kindness to someone who needs it,
   that's an act of worship.

When you write someone a letter to encourage them or sit down
and open your Bible with someone to teach them,
   that's an act of worship.

*This is my prayer for you: that your love will grow more and more;
that you will have knowledge and understanding with your love;
. . . that you will do many good things with the help of Christ to bring
glory and praise to God.* PHILIPPIANS 1:9, 11

Come into his city

with songs of thanksgiving

and into his courtyards

with songs of praise.

Thank him and praise

his name.

PSALM 100:4

Our biblical act of worship is not what we do on Sunday mornings in ties and dresses, but our act of worship is a lifelong, seven-days-a-week process of placing ourselves upon an altar of sacrifice. Worship is living the principles of Christ in everything we do. You're worshiping God by what you do all week long.

The whole purpose of coming before the King is to praise him, to live in recognition of his splendor. Praise—lifting up our heart and hands, exulting with our voices, singing his praises—is the occupation of those who dwell in the kingdom.

Then I heard all creatures in heaven and on earth and under the earth and in the sea saying: "To the One who sits on the throne and to the Lamb be praise and honor and glory and power forever and ever."
REVELATION 5:13

God is an exalted friend, a holy Father, and an elevated King. How do we approach him—as king, as father, or as friend? The answer: yes!

I love the Lord,

because he listens to my prayers for help.

He paid attention to me, so I will call to him

for help as long as I live.

PSALM 116:1-2

Those who win the victory will sit with me on my throne in the same way that I won the victory and sat down with my Father on his throne.

REVELATION 3:21

I believe that praise and prayer develop us for what we will do when we arrive in heaven. What's your picture of what you'll be doing there—sitting on a cloud? Polishing your halo? Playing your harp? That's not what you're going to be doing. You're going to be involved in the ongoing process of coreigning with God.

Strength from the Shepherd

We have a Father who is filled with compassion, a feeling Father who hurts when his children hurt. We serve a God who says that even when we're under pressure and feel like nothing is going to go right, he's waiting for us, to embrace us whether we succeed or fail.

As the mountains surround Jerusalem, the Lord

surrounds his people now and forever.

PSALM 125:2

No one is useless to God. No one, at any point in his life, is useless to God—not a little child, not the unattractive, not the clumsy, not the tired, not the discouraged. God uses his children.

God does not see the same way people see.
People look at the outside of a person,
but the Lord looks at the heart.
1 SAMUEL 16:7

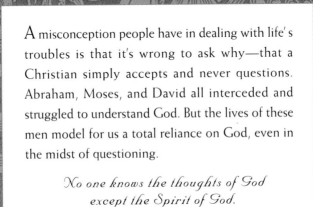

A misconception people have in dealing with life's troubles is that it's wrong to ask why—that a Christian simply accepts and never questions. Abraham, Moses, and David all interceded and struggled to understand God. But the lives of these men model for us a total reliance on God, even in the midst of questioning.

No one knows the thoughts of God
except the Spirit of God.
1 CORINTHIANS 2:11

It's not a sin to doubt. Disbelief is sin, but questioning—

sincerely seeking—is acceptable to God because in the

presence of God you may ask any question you want.

But I will call to God for help, and the Lord will save me. Morning, noon, and night I am troubled and upset, but he will listen to me.

PSALM 55:16-17

You know when I sit down and when I get up.

You know my thoughts before I think them.

You know where I go and where I lie down.

You know thoroughly everything I do.   PSALM 139:2-3

Perhaps the reason that God doesn't always give us the answer to the *whys* of our existence is that he knows we haven't got the capacity to understand the answer. In learning to depend on God, we must accept that we may not know all the answers, but we know *who* knows the answers.

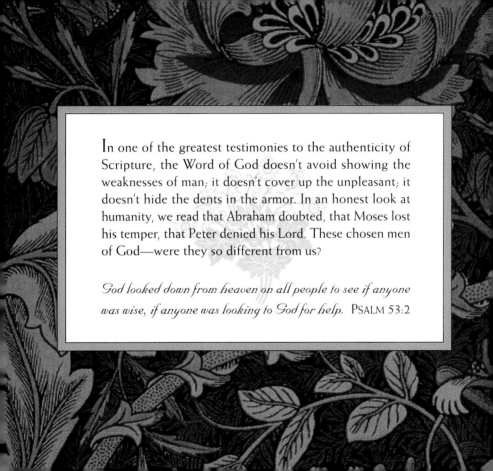

In one of the greatest testimonies to the authenticity of Scripture, the Word of God doesn't avoid showing the weaknesses of man; it doesn't cover up the unpleasant; it doesn't hide the dents in the armor. In an honest look at humanity, we read that Abraham doubted, that Moses lost his temper, that Peter denied his Lord. These chosen men of God—were they so different from us?

God looked down from heaven on all people to see if anyone was wise, if anyone was looking to God for help. PSALM 53:2

This man was born blind

so that God's power

could be shown in him.

JOHN 9:3

Jesus and his disciples were walking down the road
when they saw a blind man. The disciples said, "Jesus,
who sinned?" Jesus said, "No one sinned." Then Jesus
healed the man. And he answered once and for all that
our pain is not a result of our sin. God is not so small
that he would zap us when we make a mistake. In fact,
this passage teaches just the opposite: Our Savior is not
asleep; our Savior is alive and interested in our pain.

The Lord is my light and
the one who saves me. I fear no one.
The Lord protects my life;
I am afraid of no one.
PSALM 27:1

The Christian in the midst of a crisis

doesn't allow everyone's opinion or

everyone's feelings to cause him to

drift away from what is most

important. He sets his anchor deep in

the Word and firm in his faith.

Don't be afraid of what they fear; do not dread those things.

1 PETER 3:14

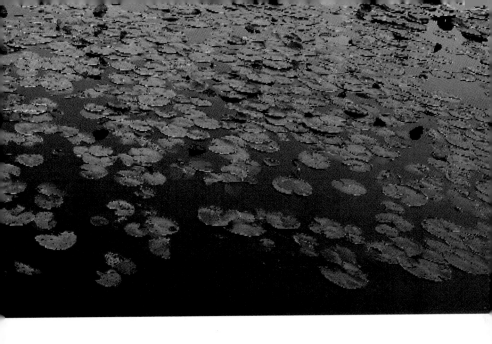

Jesus is not afraid of the things that cause us fear. He never said, "Don't bring your fears to me; I'm too busy." Instead, he said, "I'm not afraid of the things that cause you fear. Bring your fears to me."

Our fight is not against people on earth
but against the rulers and authorities and the
powers of this world's darkness, against the
spiritual powers of evil in the heavenly world.
EPHESIANS 6:12

Where's our battleground in life? Is our battle against our neighbor?

Is our battle against our family? No. The battle is with the invisible

forces of darkness, the evil one who has invaded the earth, whose goal

is to win the battle within every Christian. Satan failed in his desire

to control God, and it's only with God's help that we can defeat him.

Give your worries to the Lord,

and he will take care of you. He will

never let good people down.

PSALM 55:22

Only you can surrender your concerns to the

Father. No one else can take those away and give

them to God. Only you can cast all your anxieties

on the one who cares for you. What better way to

start the day than by laying your cares at his feet?

> *God's power*
> *protects you*
> *through your faith*
> *until salvation is*
> *shown to you at the*
> *end of time.*
> 1 PETER 1:5

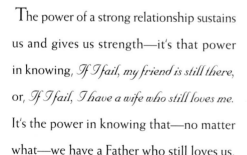

The power of a strong relationship sustains us and gives us strength—it's that power in knowing, *If I fail, my friend is still there,* or, *If I fail, I have a wife who still loves me.* It's the power in knowing that—no matter what—we have a Father who still loves us.

Praying in the Power of the Spirit

Father, when you were on earth, you prayed. You prayed

in the morning, you prayed at night, you prayed alone,

you prayed with people. In your hours of distress you

retreated into times of prayer. In your hours of joy you

lifted your heart and hands to the Father in prayer. Help

us to be more like you in this way . . . help us to make

prayer a priority in our daily lives.

Continue praying, keeping alert,
and always thanking God.
COLOSSIANS 4:2

When Jesus talks about prayer, he doesn't present it as an arduous task, he doesn't describe it as a requirement, he doesn't say that it's something you do and hopefully beautifully so that some divine audience will throw flowers to you. That's not what prayer is. It's the divine relationship that allows us to stand before God and express the deepest concerns of our hearts.

But dear friends, use your most holy faith to build yourselves up, praying in the Holy Spirit.
JUDE 1:20

So I bow in prayer before the Father from whom every family in heaven and on earth gets its true name. I ask the Father in his great glory to give you the power to be strong inwardly through his Spirit. I pray that Christ will live in your hearts by faith and that your life will be strong in love and be built on love.

EPHESIANS 3:14-17

Prayer is the recognition that if God had not engaged himself in our problems, we would still be lost in the blackness. It is by his mercy that we have been lifted up. Prayer is that whole process that reminds us of who God is and who we are.

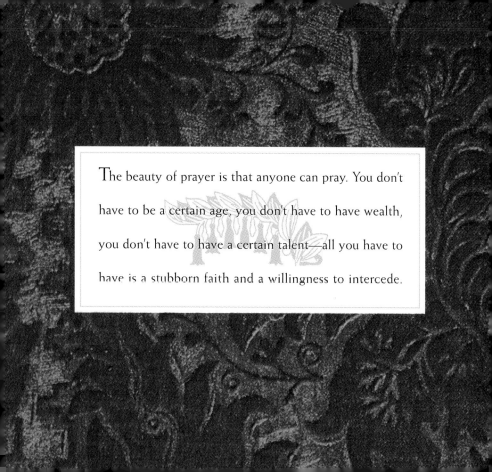

The beauty of prayer is that anyone can pray. You don't have to be a certain age, you don't have to have wealth, you don't have to have a certain talent—all you have to have is a stubborn faith and a willingness to intercede.

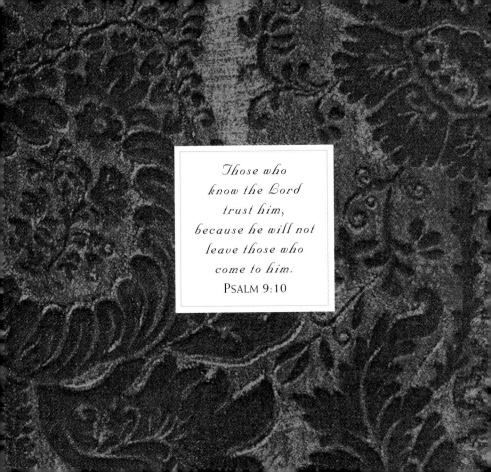

Those who
know the Lord
trust him,
because he will not
leave those who
come to him.

PSALM 9:10

I believe there's great power in prayer. I believe God heals the wounded and that he can raise the dead. But I don't believe we tell God what to do and when to do it. You see, there's a difference between faith and presumption. There's a difference between believing he's the almighty God and demanding that he become our divine servant.

The Lord shows his true love every day. At night I have a song, and I pray to my living God.

PSALM 42:8

In our "bootstrap" society, where you tough it out and do it on your own and take pride in being a rugged individualist, the one thing that seems to escape us is being before God on our knees, being before God aware that we are helpless, and *allowing* him to assist us.

Let us, then, feel very sure that we can come before God's throne where there is grace. There we can receive mercy and grace to help us when we need it.

HEBREWS 4:16

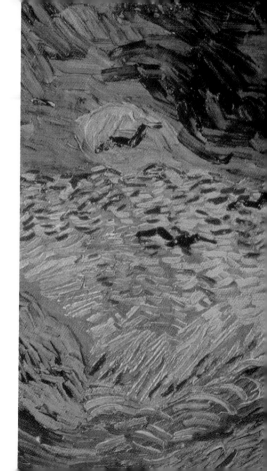

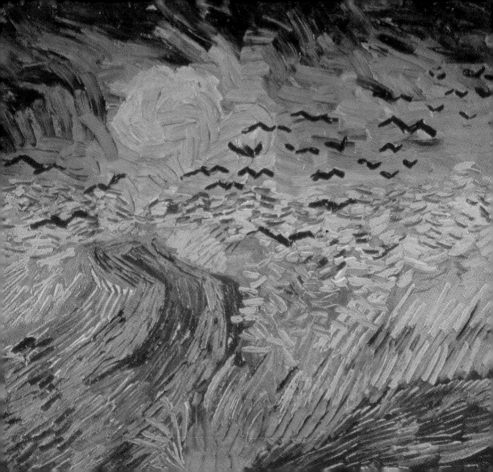

The Christian is the one who seeks to discern the voice of God amidst the many voices that come our way. One of the greatest challenges that we have is to learn to hear the voice of truth.

Let us look only to Jesus, the One who began our faith and who makes it perfect.

HEBREWS 12:2

Then people will say,
"There really are rewards for doing what is right.
There really is a God who judges the world."
PSALM 58:11

Listen to the voice of Christ rather than to the voices of men. Jesus says you can't please men and still be a servant of God. Those who listen and follow Christ will be received into heaven by the pierced hands of the one who knows the freedom of giving up what you cannot own in order to receive what no one can take from you—eternal life.

God knows that with our limited vision we don't even know that for which we should pray. And we are praying for things right now that God knows would not be best for us. When we entrust our requests to him, we trust him to honor our prayers with holy judgment.

Answer me when I pray to you, my God who does what is right. Make things easier for me when I am in trouble. Have mercy on me and hear my prayer. PSALM 4:1

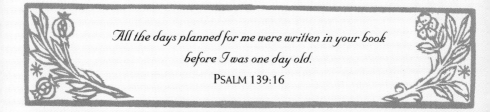

All the days planned for me were written in your book
before I was one day old.

PSALM 139:16

You know, we really don't know what to pray for,
do we? What if God had answered every prayer that you
ever prayed? Just think who you'd be married to. Just think
where you'd be living. Just think what you'd be doing.

Those who go to God Most High for
safety will be protected by the
Almighty. I will say to the Lord, "You
are my place of safety and protection.
You are my God and I trust you."

PSALM 91:1-2

Listen to the counsel of God, reestablish your roots, and pray.
This is the only way to achieve safe passage through a crisis in your life.

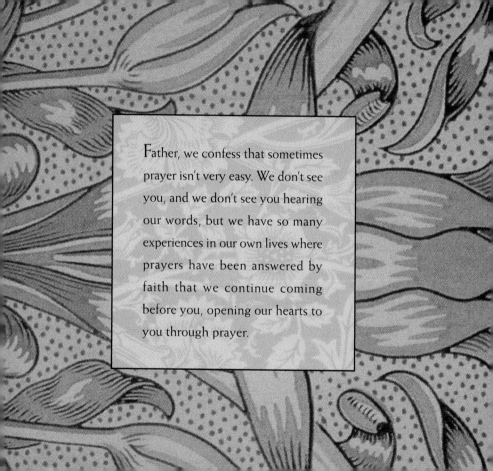

Father, we confess that sometimes prayer isn't very easy. We don't see you, and we don't see you hearing our words, but we have so many experiences in our own lives where prayers have been answered by faith that we continue coming before you, opening our hearts to you through prayer.

Lord, every morning
you hear my voice.
Every morning, I tell you
what I need, and
I wait for your answer.

PSALM 5:3

Walking with the Savior

Most of the people in the world have never seen the

When Jesus saw

Jesus of the New Testament—a Redeemer whose eyes

Mary crying and

would swell with tears and whose heart would beat

the Jews who came

with passion. Most people serve a Redeemer only when

with her also

they need a favor—a sort of magic Lord who's ignored

crying, he was

except in time of crisis. We can't imitate that kind of

upset and was

Jesus. But the tenderhearted Jesus of the New Testament

deeply troubled.

demands imitation by those who follow him.

JOHN 11:33

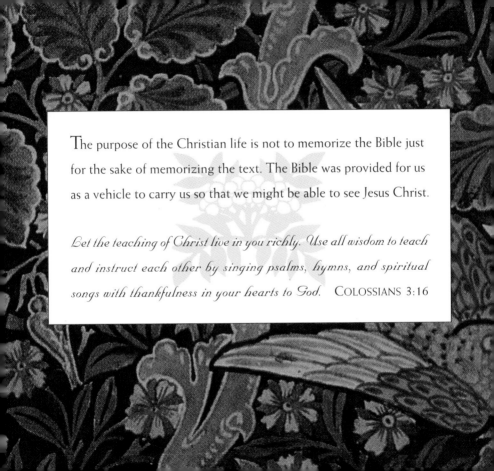

The purpose of the Christian life is not to memorize the Bible just for the sake of memorizing the text. The Bible was provided for us as a vehicle to carry us so that we might be able to see Jesus Christ.

Let the teaching of Christ live in you richly. Use all wisdom to teach and instruct each other by singing psalms, hymns, and spiritual songs with thankfulness in your hearts to God. COLOSSIANS 3:16

As you received
Christ Jesus the Lord,
so continue to live in him.
Keep your roots deep in him
and have your lives
built on him.

COLOSSIANS 2:6-7

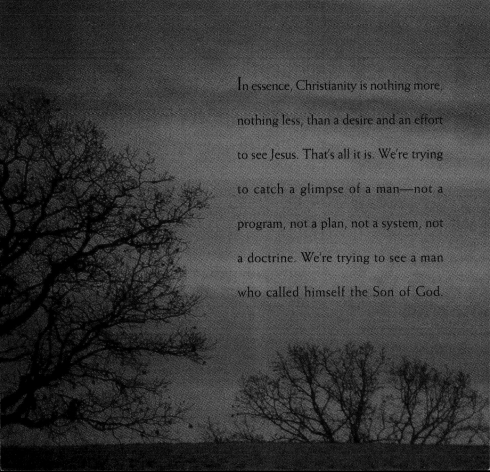

In essence, Christianity is nothing more, nothing less, than a desire and an effort to see Jesus. That's all it is. We're trying to catch a glimpse of a man—not a program, not a plan, not a system, not a doctrine. We're trying to see a man who called himself the Son of God.

Don't retire your brain when you become a follower of Christ. Be a thinker. Jesus told his followers to be shrewd as snakes. The first thing you need to do to solve problems is to get your brain in gear! That may not sound very spiritual, but it's a very practical principle. You need to use your head.

Listen, I am sending you out like sheep among wolves.
So be as smart as snakes and as innocent as doves.

MATTHEW 10:16

A Christian in his surroundings should encourage everyone to be better, instead of being the one who stoops to be like everyone else.

My dear brothers and sisters, I love you and want to see you. You bring me joy and make me proud of you, so stand strong in the Lord as I have told you.

PHILIPPIANS 4:1

The wise people will shine like the brightness of the sky.
Those who teach others to live right will shine
like stars forever and ever.
DANIEL 12:3

Do you ever get tired or bored with your work? Christ says to turn your work into a ministry—don't let it be just a vocation. Reach out to people. Let your time at work be a source of joy and encouragement to others, and you'll find greater personal joy and satisfaction as well.

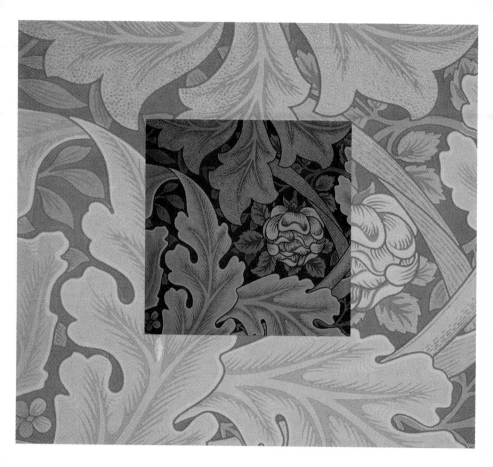

The Lord defends those who suffer;
he defends them in times of trouble.
PSALM 9:9

Does the rubble of your life take you off course and cause frustration?
Get rid of the rubble—sit down and organize your day, decide where
to start and where to finish. Sometimes we think that being a Christian
means saying yes to every request that comes our way. But sometimes
you are being more faithful by being disciplined and knowing where
to use your gifts. Put your strength on your strengths.

Perhaps the seeds sown by you in your areas of conflict won't reach maturity tomorrow or next week or even for a generation. But does that mean you shouldn't sow the seeds? No! It means you should sow the seeds *immediately*. Never underestimate the power of a seed of peace sown by a peacemaker: the power of a kind word, a seed of apology, a phone call, an explanation. This is the way we serve a God of peace.

I am the Lord your God, who teaches you to do what is good, who leads you in the way you should go. If you had obeyed me, you would have had peace like a full-flowing river. ISAIAH 48:17-18

Lord, let me live so people will praise you.
PSALM 143:11

Do what is right this week, whatever it is, whatever comes down the path, whatever problems and dilemmas you face— just do what's right. Maybe no one else is doing what's right, but you do what's right. You be honest. You take a stand. You be true. After all, regardless of what you do, God does what is right: He saves you with his grace.

Conflict is inevitable, but combat is optional.

Use your God-given creative energy to resolve

conflict before it escalates into combat.

Do to others

what you would want

them to do to you. . . .

Then you will have

a great reward,

and you will be children of

the Most High God.

LUKE 6:31, 35

Plant goodness, harvest the fruit of loyalty, plow the new ground of knowledge. Look for the Lord until he comes and pours goodness on you like water. HOSEA 10:12

Father, help us to use our time wisely, to take advantage

of the opportunities we have to be just the type of

Christians  you want us

to be. When it seems like

we don't have enough time

to do what we need to do, increase our gratitude for

the challenges of each day. And help us meet those

challenges in ways that will please you.